I0436642

The Ultimate Minimalist Guide to Declutter and Simplify Your Life in 7 Days

by Neo Monefa

Table of Contents

1. Introduction
2. What Is Minimalism?
3. The Origin Of Minimalism
4. The Modern Day Minimalist
5. How To Live A Minimalist Lifestyle?
6. Pros And Cons Of Minimalism
7. Minimalism and Green Lifestyle
8. Tidying Up and Decluttering Your Life
9. Minimalism Tips
10. Minimalism Action Plan
11. Conclusion

12. THANK YOU FOR FOR READING!

1. Introduction

Almost everyone is busy chasing lives a bit too fast. Have you ever really stopped and asked yourself as to what is it that you are chasing? We have all become so blinded by the need to get more and then some more that we end up robbing ourselves of the inner peace and tranquility.

This brings us to the topic of minimalism which will be our agenda of discussion. In this book, I am going to give you a thorough insight of what minimalism is and how you can live that lifestyle. So, all those of you who do not have a clear picture of this way of life, this is your chance to understand the particulars and even try your hand at this lifestyle.

There are a lot of perks of following the minimalistic lifestyle as it will help you get rid of the clutter in your life and make you appreciate the things you have. Most people who have completed this lifestyle method have managed to reap significant dividends. So, now is your turn to benefit from it.

2. What Is Minimalism?

"Simplicity is often the best form of beauty."

Some people tend to confuse minimalism with an absolutely simple living. While there is some relation between the two terms, but it is wrong to use them interchangeably. Ideally, minimalism refers to the art of living wherein people need to find out the things and stuff that assume the highest importance and to prioritize them. At the same time, it is important to get rid of the useless clutter which might not serve any need.

You don't need to give up on every possible luxury and minimalistic lifestyle doesn't mean that you have to live like a poor man. It is all about living a life on purpose and to live more with less. Of course, there are a lot of overlapping definitions and different people will give you varying perspectives on the term.

Is It A Lifestyle?

Yes, minimalism is a form of lifestyle wherein those who are practicing it will aim to get rid of the unwanted clutter which is present in their life. These days, it seems that a lot of people end up living a life wherein they didn't even know what they are doing.

Think of a situation wherein you have just too much stuff- say clothes you don't wear, the equipment you never used, the stuff you don't even know where it is and all the fancy products which serve no use whatsoever to you. You might not even know where the stuff is and in such cases, you will not utilize everything you have.

Does it really make any sense to do any unwanted waste? Definitely not! This is where the heart of minimalism lies. Minimalism is based on the principles of making lives a lot simpler and helping you to learn the art of efficient optimization so that you can push your life in the right direction.
So, coming back to our original question – yes it is indeed a lifestyle. It is a form of living where you slowly learn how to let go of your

desire to possess more stuff than what you need. Minimalism works on the principle of embracing the need to have things that are necessary for your day to day life and to create a fine line and demarcate the stuff you won't really need.

Not everyone can adopt this form of living, but when you are willing to put in your very best and you have the right guide, it gets easier to follow this approach.

Now that you have the basic initial idea about what minimalism is, we are going to add to the right details and by the end of this book, you will be all set to follow this style of living and thereby make the most of your life.

Are you all set to kick start? We do not take 'no' for an answer.

3. The Origin Of Minimalism

Minimalism has its root in a lot of different places. You can find its use spread in various fields. It is hard to get a clear idea of when exactly this thought process came into being. However, it took the shape of a movement.

It was back in the mid-sixties that the term became a bit popular. Soon, a lot of people were talking about the need to keep things simpler and yet effective. It was a new concept and something that was radically different than how most people perceived life to be.

However with time, there were a lot of people who could see and understand the depth of the details. It is then that they realized that it was important to adapt a different kind of lifestyle and the growth of minimalism began. Minimalism became more than just a way of living as its influence was found in several fields, ranging from arts to music, design and more.

People everywhere started chanting the need to follow a simpler approach rather than fuss it with too many things.

The Spiritual Connection

There are a lot of people who debate that the origin of minimalism can be traced back to spiritual books. Christians believe that Jesus always proclaimed the need to live a simple life. Similarly, the Sharman traditions from the Iron Age India also talk of a similar theory as they emphasized the need to live a simple life.

There are leaders like Confucius, Buddha, and Laozi who have all spoken along the same lines and this is why there are people who believe that the base of this principle can be attributed to the teachings of these leaders.

Of course, there is no definite line and the concept seemed to have evolved over time. Regardless of where the theory exactly originated and who are the founding fathers of it, one cannot undermine the fact that it is one of the most effective of all theories. It is something which needs to be implemented by a larger amount of people.

With the whopping amount of waste that is generated and the needless lavishness which too many people opt for, minimalism is slowly becoming more of a necessity than an option.

More and more people need to be educated about the importance of sticking to a simpler style of life, after all, being simple doesn't mean that you would be deprived of the things you need.
Still in doubts as to what does living life as a minimalist mean? Let us take a look at the core details.

4. The Modern Day Minimalist

Ideally, you do not need to be a rocket scientist to know what minimalism truly means, but even then owing to a lot of overlapping definition and a lot of flawed theories, it is important to give you a precise picture of the key principles which forms the basis of modern day minimalism.

There is no doubt that almost every concept and theory tends to change a little over a period of time because you need to adjust along with the change which comes in the society. The minimalistic theory that pertains to the modern day living is based upon some of these key aspects.

Own Only What You Need

Even little children these days seem to have a huge list of the stuff they need. The moment there is a new Smartphone released in the market, you may crave to buy it, even when your current one works perfectly fine. So, if you give in to your greed and buy the new phone, what happens to the old one? It becomes useless.

This is exactly what you should not do when you are following the modern minimalistic lifestyle. It is not about living the life of a poor, but to know the stuff that you need and to make a life with these items.

Cutting The Clutter

Despite your best efforts, almost each one of us will have some kind of clutter. These are the useless stuff that takes up room in your life but does not serve any need. Now, one of the most important thing to add here is that sometimes the clutter isn't just things, but a lot of useless relations, emotions and people as well.

You need to really sit down and think about what you want from your life. Think of all the things which you need for being happy and the ones that do not really matter. When you can draw this chart, you will be able to separate the clutter from your basic needs and this, in turn, can help you live the life of a modern minimalistic.

Be Mobile

One of the key aspects of living a modern minimalistic lifestyle is to stay mobile. Those who do not have a lot of useless and wanted stuff with them will find it extremely easy to move from one place to another. You do not have to worry about all the endless stuff which you need to shuffle.

So, a modern day minimalistic is one who will be able to get rid of the junk in his/her life, no matter whether it is a thing or even emotions and people and live the kind of life which is simple yet infuses him/her with happiness.

There are plenty of long-term perks of living such a lifestyle and over a period of time, you will begin to appreciate the healthy changes which it will bring in your life.

Keep Your Focus On

This is one of the buzzwords when it comes to modern day minimalistic lifestyle. When you just start practicing it, you might find it very hard to stay focused. In life, you will often come across a lot of temptation. Often, the urge to buy stuff which is just appealing, but doesn't really serve any use can be very high. However, you need to know that not all desires should be indulged in.

It is important for you to be sure that you can stay focused and then you will be able to work upon the dynamics of how to control your temptation. The more you understand the details of sticking to your idea; the better will be your approach.

These are the key points which define the life of a modern minimalist. We are not asking you to give up on every possible marvel of technology and live life like a sage, vagabond or a nomad. However, you will have to draw a line.

- Don't own too many fancy cars when you rarely travel.

- Don't buy too many cosmetics when you don't even wear makeup.

What is the point of having hundreds of toys, most of which your child won't even play with twice? They simply add to the clutter and will keep you away from the right style of living.

So, you need to once again sit down and spot the toys and games which you need for your child. Ideally, you should keep the ones which will help your children in improving their motor skills and then get rid of the rest.

You might think that it isn't much initially, but every clutter that you get rid of is a step in the right direction. It will ultimately help you be sure that you will be able to master the art of living a minimalistic lifestyle.

3.   Too Much Television

Honestly, ask yourself how many hours do you spend on the television? Do you even get anything concrete out of it? What use will it serve, if at all? This is why you need to assess the need to have too many televisions in your room.

As per a research, it has been found that on an average, an American home has more television sets than people. Isn't this a terrible statistic! It makes you wonder how much useless stuff we tend to buy. More so, most of the reality shows are useless. Television is not going to help you improve your intellectuality and there are very few shows which actually contribute to your improved understanding.

So, try to get rid of too many televisions and at the same time, cut down your viewing hours too. When you manage to do so, it will help you improve your output in ways more than one.

4.   Furniture

This is perhaps the worst of all clutter. There are so many homes which have a lot of useless furniture. The idea of having furniture is to keep stuff organized and clean, but when there is just too much of furniture; does it really serve any need? We have seen that too much of furniture simply eats into your space. Try to clear some of the unwanted furniture which is just acting as a space holder and you will be amazed at how much space will be cleared.

As per various psychological studies, it has been found that human brains operate the best in open atmospheres and spacious rooms. If your room is already too cluttered and jam-packed with just too much furniture, it is not going to help you function healthily.

So, starting today, look at the furniture pieces you don't need and be all set to get rid of them.

Just like the furniture in your home, there may be a lot of fancy interiors decor stuff as well. These are yet another unnecessary addition which serves no need. You will need to find out the useless clutter which is present in your home and get rid of it.

Your home doesn't needs to look like a museum and not everything seems to be put on display. So, the best thing which you can do is look out for decor which is sure to help your home look beautiful. Get rid of the unwanted mess and you will begin to appreciate the need to adapt to a minimalistic lifestyle.

5. Kitchen And Countertops

Women, in particular, tend to have a thing for filling their kitchen with a lot of unnecessary stuff. From three kinds of fancy juicers to the latest microwave oven and what not, your kitchen can be one huge mess.

Not just the utensil and kitchen equipment, but even too many drawers and countertops add to the fuss. So, when you are all set to adapt to a minimalistic lifestyle, you will have to be sure that you can get rid of the unwanted stuff.

Take a detour of your kitchen and assess the supplies. Upon efficient and thorough analysis, you are sure to find a lot of unwanted stuff which is simply present in your kitchen but doesn't really add any value to it.

This was a list of five of the top ways by which you can start your journey of living a minimalistic lifestyle. Of course, there are a lot more things which you need to do.

The central idea is to get in the groove and then you can keep on following it. Most people who have adopted this form of lifestyle have confessed that it is the first step which is the toughest.

When you begin the journey, you will start appreciating the way things look a lot better with less clutter and then you can proceed and apply the same logic to other parallels and thereby simplify your life in an apt manner.

6. Pros And Cons Of Minimalism

When it comes to living a minimalistic lifestyle, there have been both sides of the argument. While there are people who vouch for it, you will also come across a lot of people who will make you question the need to choose such a form of living.

In order to help you come to your own unbiased judgment, we are here to sort out the trouble by showing you both sides of the story. When you are well versed with both the pros and cons of minimalism, it will be easier for you to decide whether or not to go for it and what it expect when you embrace this new form of living.

The Pros Of Minimalism

1. Happier Life

Of course, you will live a happier life. There are a lot of us who equate happiness with money and luxuries, but if you sit down and brood, happiness is not about being able to afford the fancy luxuries or going to some of the most exotic destination in your private jet. If this was what happiness meant, would you find so many celebs battling depression? Happiness is an inside job and when you are contented with the little you have and you adapt to a minimalistic way of living, you are a lot likely to be much happier.

2. Less expenses

Yet another thing you need to know is that as minimalistic lifestyle professes the principles of living a life with less, this automatically mans that you will end up making huge savings. No matter what you buy, it costs you some money and a lot of times, we end up buying stuff we don't need. Minimalist works on the principle of not splurging on stuff you won't need. So, this will actually help you in making substantial savings and in the long run, it is sure to help you capitalize your savings a great deal.

3. Less distractions

Of course, when you are looking to live a minimalistic lifestyle, you will be able to get rid of too many distractions. The more the stuff in your life, the greater will the amount of distraction. You may not realize but distractions tend to hinder your progress and it will end up impacting the overall efficiency which you have.

When you have too many things on your mind, your work output is going to deplete and so would be the ease with which you can enjoy your life. So, by choosing to opt for a minimalistic lifestyle, you can get rid of the distractions extensively and this, in turn, will help you out in ways more than one.

These are three of the prime benefits which people with minimalistic lifestyle enjoy. Of course, there are a lot of other related benefits like improved health when you follow the minimalist diet, longer lifespan (hopefully) and a plethora of other things.

But, not everything is great as there are downsides to every aspect. You would be missing out on a few important things by choosing the minimalistic way of life. Here are few of the cons that one should keep in mind before getting rid of all the unnecessary clutter from their life.

1. It can get confusing

There is no rule book that can define the essential set of steps that one should follow in order to truly attain a minimalistic life. It can get confusing at times to choose a barometer of the kind of lifestyle you want. You can read the stories of other people who are living the same way of life and can't stop from contemplating on the difference of standards. Without a set of rules, it can get a little distracting and overwhelming at the time, not knowing what is to be done.

2. Lethargic

It has been observed that only a few days after attaining a minimalist lifestyle, people get lethargic. When they cut their connection from the outer world, their will to truly go out and get in touch with nature also diminishes at the time. Laziness is one of the most prominent disadvantages of choosing a minimalist lifestyle that should be avoided.

To make sure that you don't get extremely lethargic, go out and be with your friends and family. Explore the world and travel in your own way. There can be a thousand reasons for you to go out and have a great time with your friends. To make sure that you don't fall into the vicious circle of laziness, keep an eye on your move and try to find happiness in every little thing that the world has to offer.

3. Uniformity

After a certain point of time, you might get bored of the same limited set of things by your side. Every day might turn out to be the same at times, and it might start feeling a little mundane every once in a while. All the other people who are following a minimalistic approach will look the same and it would be tough to truly stand out from the crowd. You should remember the reason to opt this kind of lifestyle was not to be identified as a unique individual in the first place. Try exploring different places and practice new skills so that monotony won't set in.

4. Misconception

A lot of time people think of a minimalistic lifestyle as poor, when in fact, it is not true at all. It is a way of life and is not related to any financial standards. Though, this is one of the misconceptions that people who have no or less idea about the lifestyle will have. When people come to your place and don't find all those fancy things in your décor, they might start thinking that you are poor. If you are choosing to live a life of a minimalist, then you should get yourself ready for a lot of questions. It won't be that easy, but it will definitely be worth it in the end.

7. Minimalism and Green Lifestyle

Often minimalistic lifestyle is associated with living a green and lean way of life. It is one of the basic human characteristics to be close to nature and embrace its raw form and minimalism certainly focuses on that one major aspect.

Appreciate the beauty

One of the best things about minimalistic lifestyle is that it gives you a whole new perspective of the world that you live in. Letting you appreciate the beauty of nature, it encourages you to live in the moment and harness the rawness of nature as its best form. A life is not about merely existing, but it is about making sure that each and every moment has been counted at its best and creating memories on the go, which is exactly what minimalism aims for.

When we refer to the beauty of nature, we not only imply the panoramic view from the top of the mountain or the essence of a freshly blossomed flower. It is about getting in touch with nature and embracing it in every possible way – from the lush green mountains to huge waterfalls.

Carbon Footprint and Green Lifestyle

It has been noticed that people who practice the minimalistic way of living results in a better (and substantially smaller) scale of the carbon footprint than those who don't. Carbon footprint is a collective measure of every individual's consumption of natural resources to support their lifestyle. Since minimalism doesn't require an individual to gain a lot of fancy stuff that only deteriorates nature, their carbon footprint also decreased\s drastically. In order to attain the green lifestyle, minimalism is the right way to go. It will not only bring you closer to nature, but will also encourage you to feel it like never before. You would be a great example for others and might end up inspiring others to be more concerned about the Earth.

Following are some ways that help with the concept of minimalism and green lifestyle:

- By getting a smaller place to live, you can choose to have a bigger garden and include trees in your area, which will result in a better oxygen level for your surroundings.

- Most of the people who follow a minimalistic lifestyle don't have a vehicle. Taking a public transit or riding a bicycle can help a lot to attain a green lifestyle.

- Wearing non-designer clothes will not only cost you less, but will also improve the quality of fauna and flora around the world.

- The diet of most the minimalistic people involves fruits and seasons vegetable. You might start growing your own food or can get them from a local farmer's market, which will help you attain a greener lifestyle.

Understanding the concept of minimalism and connecting it to the green way of living is a subjective one. Once you start living this new way of life, you will have to make choices every day that will not only define you as an individual, but will certainly bring you closer to nature too.

8. Tidying Up and Decluttering Your Life

Minimalism could be of great help to declutter your life and organize everything from your house to your surroundings in a better way. After a while, you will feel the difference in your actions and almost everything you do. It will create that much-needed breathing space in your life, letting you build the best lifestyle for yourself.

The Art of Letting Go

Minimalism will teach you the art of letting go. When you will take the high road, there would be instances when you would be asked to let go of your favorite dresses or some precious belongings. It is only after letting them go, you would realize that you never wanted it in the first place.

Minimalism will make you let go of the things that you don't need in your life anymore, helping you create a clean space around you. Who doesn't like a clean wardrobe, a decluttered house, or an organized life? With minimalism, you can have it all while mastering the art of letting go and having only the essential things by your side.

A Clean Space

With less furniture and other items at your place, it would make it extremely easy for you to clean it without any trouble. You will utilize your energy in better things like taking care of your body and making your surroundings neat and clean. Minimalism will let you keep only the set of essential things that you need. With this kind of practice, you can choose to have a cleaner space around you.

From your bed to your living space, there won't be any scope of clutter at all. Usually, when we clean our home and remove all the clutter, chances are that place gets dirty again after a few days. But when you are following a minimalistic way of living, you simply need to declutter your place once and the chances of that mess coming back to your house diminishes drastically.

Decluttering your Life

Minimalism is not only about having a cleaner space around you, but it also helps you to organize your life in a better way. Minimalism will put you closer to nature and invoke the spiritual guru in you. After a while, you will get to figure out what matters in your life and what not. What are the things that should be your priorities and what never mattered! The lifestyle can teach you a lot by setting your goals and making you realize what really matters in your life.

Your new way of lifestyle will make you a better organizer. You will start setting new goals and will see how easily you would be able to accomplish them. It might make you shrink your circle and social space, but it would be a great thing as you will get to see who really matters in your life. You will end up having a close knit of friends in your circle, who will always stay with you for better or worse. You will start finding happiness in small things and will find solace in the truest form of life.

9. Minimalism Tips

In order to truly attain the raw essence of minimalism lifestyle in your life, it is essential that you make yourself ready to welcome this change. Any significant change in life can be tough at first, but after following a rigorous routine and following some tips, it can easily be attained.

Congratulate yourself for choosing this great way of living. Now when you are ready to commence a minimalistic way of living, follow these hand-picked tips that can help you welcome minimalism to your life in a better way. Hop on and try to inculcate these tips and get amazed by their results.

1. Use it or lose it

Yes, it is as simple and easy as it sounds. This is the thumb rule to attain minimalism. It doesn't matter if you are cleaning your wardrobe or your store room, or if you are trying to make big decisions like moving to another smaller space or keeping your old house, this rule will help you substantially to decide what you want. Simply ask yourself, whether you would be using it for the coming years and on a constant basis or not. If the answer is "no", then there is no point of keeping it. Lose it before it starts to make a clutter in your space.

2. Start Small

Minimalism lifestyle can bring a crucial change to your life and should not be attained at once. Remember that Rome was not built in a day and if you really want to bring a healthy change in your life then start by taking simple steps. Take small measures and bring a change to your house and surrounding one by one, in a sequential way. Start from your wardrobe and move from one room to another. Plan your day accordingly and get rid of the things you don't want in your life anymore by taking it a step at a time.

3. Stop Procrastinating

A change won't come into your life until and unless you allow it to. Stop procrastinating things and take full control of your life by converting your plan to some actions.

4.   Get Inspired

We understand that it can sometimes get a little tough to change your lifestyle entirely. If you feel like giving up, then give yourself for a moment and think of the amazing future that you are going to have. With no boundaries or restriction, no troubles or worries, it all seems like a plan that can be worked on. Get inspired by the idea of the future that you have imagined and make it all worth it.

5.   Talk to People

Talk to your friends and family members who have already taken the minimalistic way of life. Search for people online and learn from their experience. It is really important to talk to people at this stage and learn from their mistakes. Get inspired by their stories and create your own without any hassle.

6.   Consume Less

Participate in green lifestyle, which is closely related to the minimalistic way of living. Try to sell your vehicle and start using public transport. Get a bicycle and travel around the town without any stress about the ongoing traffic. Start by consuming only the things you need and not everything that you want.

7.   Make a "minimalistic" wish list

Sometimes, it is good to treat yourself and get something once in a while. By turning a minimalistic person, it won't mean that you will stop treating yourself. Make a wish list, just like old times, but only include the things that you essentially need in your life. Don't get something just out of temporary joy. Think of the long run before truly compiling a wish list.

8.   Less is more

Last, but most significantly, when it comes to minimalism, always understand that less is more. You can always reuse stuff instead of getting a new one and can get the best out of everyday stuff that you already have. There are four questions that you should definitely ask yourself if you want to be a true minimalist.

- Can I eliminate it?
- Can I keep it?
- Can I reuse it?
- Can I produce it?

After asking these questions to yourself, you will get a clear idea of what should stay and what should go out of your life in order for you to attain a flawless way of minimalistic life.

10. Minimalism Action Plan

With so much of going around in the world, it becomes really tough at times to let go of everything that is keeping you attached to other materialistic things and pleasures that you really don't need in your life.

We have come up with an action plan that can let you identify the key areas that require work in your life and how you can rectify them in order to attain a flawless way of minimalistic lifestyle. Embrace minimalism with these three steps that will make you more action-oriented and bring a change to your life seamlessly.

1. Identify

It starts with a phase of self-realization. There comes a time in the life of almost every individual that makes them a question about the things they have. From those clothes that you didn't wear to an old laptop that could be of great use to someone else, we all have a lot of things that are of either no or of minimum usage for us. We often try to get rid of them, donate them, or eliminate them all together, but some or other thing stops us in between.

The identification of that urge to attain a minimalistic life should never be subsided. If you are thinking to live a simple life, then ask yourself what are the measures that can be adopted for it. Is minimalism truly for you, and will you be benefited by it in the long run?

To make sure that this is what you want, we recommend every individual to truly think about their future. Close your eyes and try to paint a day of your future in front of your eyes. If the image of a tension-free life appears in front of you, where you have time for yourself and have found peace in what you have, then you have your answer right there. This is the moment of identification. Don't let it go so easily!

2. Plan

After identifying that you want a minimalistic way of life, start by planning everything accordingly. Every day, every moment would count and you should utilize your time accordingly to make sure that you move ahead towards attaining the minimalistic lifestyle. Follow the tips that were mentioned in the previous sectors to sail through the entire process without much hassle.

Sometimes, the simplest of things can be the hardest. Planning a way to attain minimalism might seem easy, but it can turn out to be really hard, especially for beginners. Take one step at a time – one room per day, and start getting rid of the things you don't want in your life. Start by arranging your stuff and divide it into two piles – either keep or eliminate. Get rid of the stuff you won't want and master the art of letting go.

Follow your daily action plans rigorously and create your weekly and monthly action plans on the go. This is the most crucial step to let you attain minimalism in a smooth way and won't stop until and unless you are already there.

3. Action

After you have identified what you want and have also created a plan to achieve it, it is high-time to turn the action mode on. Start by first identifying age-old things that are of no usage to you. Outdated technology and old clothes are the best example of it. You know that old-aged technology and outdated gadgets would be of no use. Start by getting rid of them at first. When you have made your technical mess cleared, move to clothes and other accessories in your wardrobe!

Clearing a wardrobe can be the most time-consuming task, especially when you have to decide what to keep and what to get rid of. Start with old clothes and start eliminating other accessories like shoes and bags that you haven't used in the past. Only keep the things that you like the most and avoid keeping any designer product in your wardrobe. Minimalistic life is all about wearing simple clothes and consuming ordinary objects in an extraordinary way. Focus on comfort rather than style when you are short listing your clothes and keep cotton, linen, and other pleasing material, by getting rid of fur, animal prints, and other leather products.

After you have sorted out your wardrobe, move towards your kitchen to make sure that only the simplest and fresh ingredients should remain there. Minimalism is not only about wearing and possessing simple things, but it is about eating fresh and healthy meals. Try to avoid canned products and if possible, start a small kitchen garden in your backyard from where you can get all the essential fruits and vegetables to consume.

It can get a little tough sometimes to maintain a constant pace of actions. Take small breaks in the meantime and give yourself an afternoon nap before getting back into work. Let your actions speak and move from one room to another, one surrounding to another and one pointer in your list to another, to achieve success. You should remember that minimalism is not only about consuming less and having a fewer stuff on your plate, but it is a way of living that will teach you the importance of every little thing in your life, making you cherish it the most.

11. Conclusion

Now that you are aware of the true essence of minimalism, it won't be difficult at all to bring that much-needed change to your life. Minimalism is not just the way of cleaning your wardrobe or decluttering your space; it is a way of living and can bring a breath of fresh air to your life.

We have discussed both the pros as well as cons of choosing a minimalistic lifestyle and have also let you know how you can overcome them. Minimalistic lifestyle is best enjoyed in the company of good friends and family members with whom you are able to share your ideology and live life in a simple way at the same time. You will start noticing not only a substantial change in your finances but your health will also drastically improve. Those small and irrelevant things that don't really matter in your life will start to disappear so that you can focus on what really matters.

You will start spending time with your friends and family and will start to love the blessing of life. Minimalism will invoke the spark of spirituality in you and will get to know yourself in a better way. Minimalism will let you choose a green lifestyle of living and you will see the visible change in the world around you. Not only you will play your part in order to make this world a greener and better place, but you will be a great example to your friends and their kids as well.

If you are starting to go minimalistic, then you should congratulate yourself as you have already made the first move. Now when you have read the guide, you know how to go ahead and take small steps at a time to bring a revolutionary change in your life. We are sure that you will come out as a changed individual in the end and will be amazed to see the change in you.

Start this change today and take your step towards minimalism – a simpler and happier version of lifestyle. A way of living that can't be explained, as it should be experienced on your own.

12. THANK YOU FOR FOR READING!

Thank You so much for reading this book. If this title gave you a ton of value, It would be amazing for you to leave a <u>REVIEW</u> !

www.ingramcontent.com/pod-product-compliance
Lightning Source LLC
Chambersburg PA
CBHW030550290526
45786CB00004B/1959